Dear

Dear Graduate

Dear Graduate

A book for when we take a step forward.

Charlie McEnerney & Adam Larson

Clarkson Potter/Publishers
New York

Clarkson Potter/Publishers
An imprint of the Crown Publishing Group
A division of Penguin Random House LLC
clarksonpotter.com

Originally published in slightly different form by Adam&Co. in 2022.

Library of Congress Cataloging-in-Publication Data is on file with the publisher.

ISBN 979-8-217-03467-3
Ebook ISBN 979-8-217-03468-0

Editor: Emma Brodie | Assistant editor: Bri James
Designer: Adam Larson | Art director: Ian Dingman
Production editor: Terry Deal | Production manager: Kim Tyner

Manufactured in China

10 9 8 7 6 5 4 3 2 1

First Edition

For Adacie & Declan

When we are young, we are often asked the question...

What do you want to be when you grow up?

A difficult question—
and how is one
to know?

But what if the question wasn't, "What do you want to be?"

What if we asked...

What will you do when you grow up?

Will you design and build the structures that keep us safe and warm inside?

Will you sow seeds and grow and harvest healthy things to eat?

Will you care for our health, our bodies, our minds, and our souls?

Will you
transform numbers
and letters and
symbols into code?

Will you invent something useful that we've never seen before?

Will you grow
flowers or bring their
joy to our doors?

Will you drive
trucks and buses
and move mountains,
people, and everything
we need?

Will you juggle numbers, dishes, or bowling ball pins?

Will you stay
with your children,
to raise them and
teach them?

Will you care for the babies, toddlers, and children of those at work?

Will you rescue someone when they are in trouble?

Will you engineer and build bikes or cars or ships or space stations?

Will you measure,
stir, and bake?
Or prep, cook,
and clean?

Will you hit, throw, or bat? Or swim, lift, or ski?

Will you help
manage the power
of our water, energy,
or electricity?

Will you sing, dance, act, or create to bring beauty, emotion, and truth to our days?

Will you teach, to inspire, nurture, and share your knowledge?

Will you honor your elders, who have lived life well and shared their wisdom with you?

Will you make
a plan to contribute
to a better world, to
improve it for others?

Will you look toward the future, and take risks or chances and challenge yourself?

Will you cheer on your friends and family to succeed?

Will you mentor someone, offering guidance when they need it most?

Will you treat every other person, animal, and living thing with respect and care?

Will you remember
those who lifted
you up and helped
you become you?

Will you respect
what others choose
to do, too?

Will you consider all points of view and encourage diversity of thought?

Will you try to
see the world,
how we each live
and breathe?

Will you keep
your mind open,
listen, and learn to
understand others?

Will you keep
your mind open,
learn something
new every day?

No matter
what you
do, my wish
for you...

is that you
find dignity,

pride in
all of your
accomplishments,

and satisfaction
your whole
life through.

Congratulations!

Charles McEnerney

Charles McEnerney is a writer, musician, marketer, and, most importantly, a dad to Adacie and Declan. Throughout his career, he has worked at HBO, GBH/PBS, *Fast Company*, *Inc.*, and *MovieMaker* magazines, Seattle International Film Festival, Emerson College, The Grommet, and 826 Boston. Charlie was the singer, guitarist, and songwriter in the post-punk band Falling Stairs and is now a solo artist. He hosted and produced the Well-Rounded Radio music interview podcast for ten years. Charlie grew up in Flushing, Queens, in New York City and lives in Jamaica Plain in Boston, MA. He graduated from PS21, St. Michael's, Holy Cross High School, and NYU's Tisch School of the Arts. charlesmcenerney.com

Adam Larson

Adam Larson is an award-winning artist, creative director, designer, and illustrator. He founded the multidisciplinary brand design studio, Adam&Co., whose clients have included Beyoncé, Taylor Swift, Fleetwood Mac, Herbie Hancock, Hoka, Nike, Puma, Saucony, Converse, The Boston Public Library, The Isabella Stewart Gardner Museum, Harvard, MIT, CNN, Major League Baseball, Penguin Books, and Random House, among many others. He is the co-founding editor and art director of *Lemon* and *Wednesday* magazines. Adam grew up in Stoneham, MA, and lives in Florence, MA, with his American Bully, Rhys. He graduated from Robin Hood Elementary, Stoneham Middle School, Stoneham High School, and Syracuse University's College of Visual and Performing Arts. adamnco.com

Thank you to Patricia McEnerney, Marion Seymour, Natalie Jackvony, Kristin van Ogtrop at InkWell Management, Emma Brodie at Clarkson Potter, and Rhys.